Lost And Found

The Book Of Short Stories

Cici. B

This is a book of short stories from different periods in my life between the ages of twenty-three to twenty-nine. Unfortunately, I've had my share of devastating moments with more than one man, and for personal reasons, I've chosen to leave those men nameless throughout these pages.

I know some of these stories will be hard to read (shit, they were hard to write) but they're real people, things, feelings, and situations that I've experienced, and survived.

Brace yourselves...

There's a shitload of emotions on every page.

For all of the women
who have lost and found themselves
a million times,
only to lose and find themselves
all over again.

1

"It's like I'm over him, but I'm also ... not," she said as she drove. "It's like I'm cool with moving on, but I'm also not. I want someone new, but I also don't." She reached down beside her for the lighter that sat surrounded by coins in her cup holder and lit the cigarette she held between two of her fingers. She lowered her window a bit and blew out smoke. "It's just a weird space to be in," she continued. "I feel like I'm stuck in this weird space, and I don't know how to get myself out of it. You know?" I looked out of the window, remembering all of my own weird spaces, and nodded my head. "Trust me," I said. "I know exactly what you mean."

#It'sComplicated

I think we've all had moments
when we thought we could change a man.

Hopefully, we've all learned our lesson.

"So what do you want to do?" I asked him.
After a minute of silence he replied, "I don't know
anymore B." I swear, I wanted to throw my fucking
phone clear across the room.

Typical "us".

We always seemed to get to the point where we were so
fed up that neither of us knew what to do. Secretly, he
hoped I would walk away so he wouldn't have to be the
one to break it off, and I secretly hoped *he* would walk
away so that I wouldn't have to be the one to break it
off.

This is what insanity feels like, I thought to myself.

I was curled up in the corner of my sofa, cradling the
phone to my ear, staring at the wall. My head ached
from all of the thinking ... thoughts of how we got
here, and how *we,* became he and I.

I wasn't searching for anyone when we fell into each
other's lives—or maybe I was, I don't know anymore.
The beginning is kind of a blur.

I just know that we became *us*, and we never missed a beat. We never went a day without speaking, and no matter how busy our schedules got, we never went a week without touching.

I remember the way he touched me...
I remember the first time he touched me...

And I remember never wanting to be touched by anyone else, ever again.

I committed to him on my own.

He didn't force me, nor did he have to, but... he did make me feel like I was his, and he was mine, no matter what.

In two years, he managed to repair my heart and then break it again, maybe a thousand times.

We were a constant train wreck that, somehow, we always ended up surviving, together, hand in hand. The definition of *us* was thrilling, and exotic, but dangerous and destructive at the same time. One day we hated each other — "fuck you, don't ever talk to me again."

The next day we needed each other— "I love you, I miss you, stay with me."

We were toxic for each other, yet, brought each other peace at the same time. Makes no sense, right?

I know.

I'm still trying to make sense of it all myself.

He was dapper and smooth, but also jagged-edged and rude. I was soft and full of love, but also smart-mouthed, and quick-tempered.

I think I may have softened him up a bit, and that scared him. And I think he may have hardened me up a bit, and that scared me.

We'd have done anything for each other—that alone is dangerous, right? But the whole time, he was trying to sculpt me into something I wasn't. And admittedly, I tried to do the same to him.

Why did we do that to one another? I don't know. We both lacked something the other so desperately needed, yet, we refused to let go of each other—see what I mean? Insanity.

I would try to run away, but he'd come get me, and light a fire inside of me with his passion and affection.

Then he would try to run, but I'd find him, and drown him in my sea of sweet words, tender kisses and caresses. We were crazy in love all of the time, drunk in love many times, but most of the time...
we needed each other no matter the consequence.

I've had boyfriends. I've dated other men. But I've only ever loved two men in my life—and I was hoping that he would have been the last.

"This is so stupid." I whispered into the phone. Water was starting to fill my eyes and I had that lump in my throat. *That fucking lump.*

Fuck it, I thought. *If he's not going to do it, then I will.*

"I don't want to do this anymore." I said, my voice shaking. "I'm tired of hurting. I love you with every sense that I have, but after two years of this, it's becoming more and more obvious that love isn't enough here. So I think it's best we just go our separate ways—for good this time."

Tears were now flooding down my face at full speed and there was nothing I could do to make them stop. I desperately wanted him to say "B, no. I'm not letting you go this time. I love you, I want you to be happy, and I want to be the man who makes you happy."

But I knew those words weren't going to come out of his mouth.

"Sometimes I wish we could have met at a different time," he started. "Sometimes I sit and think of how different things could have been for us had we just met at a different time."

No shit. No shit, no shit NO SHIT.

I wanted to hang the phone up, but then again I didn't. Something inside me wanted to hang onto him a little while longer—even if that meant sitting on the phone in silence. I didn't care. I just needed a little more time. So there I sat, in silence, staring at the wall with a face covered in tears, sobbing as quietly as I could with the phone to my ear...

I sat there, in silence.

Maybe he too needed to hang onto me a little while longer, because he stayed on the other end with me without saying a word. My heart was breaking again—and it doesn't matter how many times your heart gets broken—you never get used to the pain. Ever.

Okay B, enough of this shit. If it's the end, then end it.

I wiped my face with the back of my hand and spoke up. "I guess we should hang up now. It seems neither of us have anything left to say."
A couple of seconds went by and he replied softly, "Goodbye B,"—and those words cut me deep.

"Goodbye." I quietly said back. I hit the 'end' button on my phone, and set it down beside me. I put my hands to my face, and with no one around to hear or see me, I cried loud and hard. I had to let it all out.

It was a weird feeling. Part of me felt like I was giving up on us. I felt guilty because I'm no fucking quitter at anything in life generally speaking. But another part of me was comforting my mind, with facts. And the facts were, there was nothing left for us to do.

We had exhausted all of our options.
We had reached our limit.
We had officially maxed out.

So in reality, I wasn't giving up on us, I was accepting that we didn't fit together, not anymore. He wasn't a bad person, I'd known bad people people, and he wasn't one of them. It was us, together, we were bad for each other. Maybe things *would* have been different had we met at a different time in our lives.

But here we were, in the now, fed up with not being able to get it right, fed up with being fucking complicated.

*"At least now I know exactly
what I don't want next time around."*

2

"I *was* over him." She said to me. "I was like, fuck him! Fuck him. Fuck him! I had pushed him outta my head, and was doing my thing just fine. But then, out of the blue, we ended up at the same place at the same time, and the minute we made eye contact, that was it. Just like that, I wasn't over him anymore."

I knew all too well that, yes, shit like that happens in the blink of an eye.

#Relapse

"I know I had no business letting him back in. I don't need you to tell me that. But he was familiar, and he knew me. He knew what I liked, what I loved, and what I needed. There was also no doubt in my mind that when the morning came, I'd open my eyes, see him laying there naked beside me, and I'd be fucking furious with myself—for those next couple of hours though, I just needed to be touched, caressed, and held in silence by someone who already knew me."

I woke up face buried in the pillow. I could smell him. I thought I was trippin' and maybe I had way too much to drink the night before. I lifted my head and focused my eyes.

I was in his room, in his bed.

No, no, no I thought to myself. *This can't be right.*

I looked under the sheets and saw my naked body. Reality set in deeper as I slowly turned to my left and saw him.

He had dark chocolate, flawless skin, and was laying on his stomach, shirtless, with the sheets resting a tad below the top of his boxers. I was facing the back of his head.

Sunuvabitch! I screamed in my mind.

"What's wrong," he muttered as if he had heard my thoughts.

I didn't really know what to say. I was confused, and wanted to kick my own ass for being back in his damn bed, *naked.*

"Nothing." I mumbled. I sat up with my back toward

him and rested my feet on the floor. I closed my eyes and rubbed my temples. Slowly, images of the night before began spilling into the front of my brain.

The club, music, drinks, fucking shots, *more* shots, him, the lights, my car, his apartment door, his kiss... *oh my God his kiss...* me on top of him, him on top of me...

I heard him chuckle and my flashbacks stopped.

"You okay over there B?"

I wanted to slap the shit out of him, really.

I opened my eyes and saw my stockings on the floor over by his dresser. Then I caught a hint of my skirt peeking out from under the bed. I shook my head.

"Why am I heeeeere?" I asked, my back still facing him.

Again he chuckled.

Why does he think this is funny? This isn't funny!

I hated him.

I closed my eyes again, and more flashbacks invaded my

mind—his hands all over me, my hands all over him. It was my birthday. I had gotten drunk, and I hadn't had sex since him—four months to be exact. Four strong, stand my ground, not give into temptation MONTHS. Shot to SHIT. Why? Because I was drunk, he was there, liquid courage took control and I went with it, like a fucking idiot.

"B. Are.You.Okay?" He asked again.

No, asshole. I'm not okay. I'M IN YOUR BED NAKED ONCE AGAIN.

"I'm fine. I have a headache. I need some Gatorade and an Aspirin, but I'm fine." I really didn't want to look at him, because obviously, I didn't hate him. Clearly, I still loved him. But I was pissed at myself, because for these past four fucking months, I'd been training myself to UNlove him. We had sex, and now I'd have to start my self-training all over.

I heard him get up, go to the bathroom and close the door, and I immediately darted around his bedroom like a frantic bat out of hell, searching for the rest of my clothes. Every time I found an article of clothing, I sighed and shook my head. I pulled on my stockings and skirt then I realize I had no panties on.

Did I even wear panties last night?

I kneeled down and searched under his bed while talking to myself aloud—"Oh look, there's my fucking bra. Good job B. Just perfect." As I reached for it, back into the room he came.

"Can you relax please?" He said in his stupid, calm, deep sexy voice that I loved so much I HATED it.

I yanked my bra out from under his bed, stood up—dressed only from my belly button down—and looked at him.

I was fucking frazzled.

I swiped my long black hair out of my face and sighed heavily.

"I want you to know, we are NOT falling back into our US routine, so just... I don't know how or why I'm back here. But we.. THIS..." I said as I pointed at him, then myself then at his bed, "this is not, and I mean *not* happening again. I relapsed. That's it. That's all. The End."

He stared at me, completely unmoved. He still had no shirt on. And his chest—that chest I loved so damn much—was distracting me.

Jesus, I need to get the fuck outta here fucking asap.

"B, can you seriously just relax please? It was your birthday. We hadn't seen each other in a while. I was drinking, you were drinking, and we had sex. Nothing for you to freak out over."

The sound of my phone ringing tuned me back into reality—the reality being that I was still standing in the middle of his bedroom with my tits in the air, my bra in my hand, and my shirt nowhere to be found. Plus, I had to pee, very badly. You know, that morning pee. But I didn't even want to *pee* in his house. I wanted to get in my car and drive the hell home.

Pushing past him, I followed the sound of my phone out into his living room. I found it face down on the sofa. I grabbed it and saw my best friend's name lit across the screen. "Hey Angel," I answered nonchalantly.

"Um, I have been ringing down your phone ALL morning." She was so damn loud. I instantly distanced the phone from my ear. "Where the fuck did you go last night? How the HELL did you get there in your drunken state? And WHERE the fuck are you right now?" I put my hand on my forehead and winced.

Fuck.

Now I *had* to lie. There was NO way I was going through any lectures about this shit. "I'm straight girl. I'll tell you all about it later. I'm with my mom right now so lemme call you back."— "Cool," she said, and we hung up.

Fuck. Fuck.

I looked up at the sound of him walking toward me. He had my shirt in his hand and extended it to me with a slight grin. "Think you'll need this or nah?"

I scowled at him, snatched it out of his hand and put it on.

Why the fuck am I still here?

I gathered my belongings, put on my coat, stuffed my bra in the pocket and went to the front door to slip on my heels.

"B don't be like that. You don't need to rush out of here. You can seriously just chill."

I opened the front door and looked back him, "Have a good day." I said, as I walked out and shut the door behind me.

Once I was in my car, I felt safe, but stupid at the same time. I was embarrassed, and my mind raced. I tried to remember if we'd left the party together or if I'd just shown up at his place on my own.

What the fuck.

I drove off and sped all the way home, deep in thought until I pulled into my driveway and turned the car off. I sat there, put my head on the steering wheel and cried.

I was so mad at myself man.

All that we had been through, all the shit I couldn't take anymore—I finally walked away.
I hadn't contacted him and he hadn't contacted me.
We hadn't seen each other once, and I was slowly getting over him—or so I thought— but now this.

It felt like I was right back to the day I walked away from him.

Deep breaths B. Deep breaths. Stop fucking crying.

I sat up and wiped my face.

It's not the end of the world, these things happen.
I'm not the first, and I won't be last woman on earth to
relapse.

"In a perfect world,
he would be mine and I would be his.
There wouldn't be any confusions and there
wouldn't be any mess—it would just be him
and I together in a complete bliss, happy
and in love with each other at the same time.
And you know what? Maybe perfect worlds
do exist... but maybe him and I just aren't
meant to live in any of them, together."

✗

3

"Your problem is, you ignore your intuition far too often." She said as she poured more liquor into my glass. I put my hand up to signal her from pouring too much and she stopped. "I do not ignore my intuition," I said. "Girl, yes you do. I watch you do it all the time. You're forever going out of your way to do right by other people, and it's great don't get me wrong, but at what point do you zero in on yourself and do right by you?" I lowered my eyes to my glass, "I guess sometimes I just feel like... I don't know. I don't want to be judged anymore than I already have been." — "Didn't anyone ever tell you that you'll be judged in this world, no matter what you do? So you might as well do what is best for you. Listen to yourself. Trust, *yourself*," she pleaded with me.

#SomeDreamsDoComeTrue

"I guess this is the part where I decide
if I'm going to let this shit make me
stronger, or eat away at me on the inside."

"T dreamt of fishes last night, so someone's pregnant. And it ain't me."

For the last sixteen years, our friend T has dreamt every single one of the pregnancies within our circle. I know. It sounds crazy when you hear it, but there are only two out of the six of us who don't have kids. All the rest? T dreamt of, *before* they took pregnancy tests. She was like the fucking pregnancy fortuneteller or some shit.

I sat at my desk doing online research for a book I started writing. My girl was on speakerphone, and her words dropped my hands right down to my tummy...

It was me.

I hadn't taken a test yet, but I was twelve days late for my period and my breasts were swollen and tender. I was sure I was just extra late because I was overstressed that month, but when she mentioned the fucking stupid fishes...

I knew.

I knew it was fucking me.

I was quiet as my girl rambled on and on. When she

finally realized I hadn't said a word the entire time, she yelled— "HELLLOO? Did you hear what I said? SOMEONE is pregnant. You know T and her fishes are always on point."

"It's me." I whispered.

"WHAT?!" She shrieked. "OH MY GOD! Girl are you serious? You're joking right now, you're just kidding... right???"

I really wanted it to be a joke. I wanted to be like "Hahaha, girl, early April fools!" But I couldn't. I explained to her how late my period was, and that I needed to take a test. She took a deep breath. "Fucking T man. She legit dreams everyone's pregnancies—that's crazy! If you find out you're pregnant for real, can I tell her?"

"NO." I yelled into the phone. "Don't say shit to anyone. I don't know what's going on, or what *will* go on, so just shut the fuck up about this... please." I knew she could keep a secret, so I wasn't even worried. "Okay. Okay. Jeesh. It's just crazy you know? Like... that's crazy."

Oh, it was fucking crazy alright. It was crazy and couldn't be more poorly timed. As she kept talking, I wandered off into my own mind. I remembered the night him and I were completely reckless, when normally, we were really safe. I also remember taking the morning after pill. So what the fuck was this?

This is bullshit. I'm just stressed, which is why my period is late, which is why my tits are swelling and heavy. I'm just really late.

"B? Girl. Are you listening to me?"

"Huh?" I came back to reality. "No, I'm really not. Sorry girl, lemme call you back." I hung up and sat back in my chair.

I need to take a test, I need to take a test, I need to take a fucking test right now.

I was getting hot. All of a sudden the room was a fucking sauna. I took off my sweater and rested my hands on my forehead.

Don't panic. Do not panic. Just take the test in the morning and everything will be fine.

Everything will be just fine... *right?* I couldn't wait until the morning though, so five hours, a two liter bottle of water, and a trip to the twenty-four hour drugstore later—I unwrapped the First Response test, sat on the toilet and peed on the stick.

The box said that one line meant not pregnant and two lines meant pregnant. I took some toilet paper, folded it, put it on the counter and placed the stick on top of it. I washed my hands and went to get a drink of water.

My fucking mouth was dry as fuck.

It was 3 A.M and I stood in my kitchen barefoot, in my panties and an oversized hoodie. I leaned against the counter with the cup of water in my hand, thinking.

Breathe. Just take a deep breath. You're going to walk back into that bathroom and that ugly thick ass stick is going to be negative and you're going to laugh and T's fishes are going to be for someone else.

I drank my water, put the cup in the sink, and walked back into my bathroom.

*One line means **not** pregnant, two lines mean pregnant.*

I picked up the stick and felt my knees buckle under me as two bright ass pink lines stared back at me.

MUTHERFu...FUCK. Oh my fuck. fuck fuck fuck fuck fuck.

With shaking hands, I grabbed the instructions from the box and read them again.

Maybe I read it wrong. You know?

I scanned it until I got to the part I needed.

One pink line = negative. Two pink lines = positive.

I held the stick with my other hand and stared at the two pink lines.

"MUTHERFUCKER." I screamed.

This was not happening right now. This just could *not* be happening right now.

I threw the test in the sink and sat with my back to the wall on the bathroom floor. The room was spinning, and my breath was getting shorter and shorter. I was on the verge of a panic attack. My phone was across the house somewhere, and at that point, the room was spinning so much and so quickly that I knew I wouldn't be able to get to it if I needed to call for help. *B, you need to calm the fuck down before you pass out.*

I closed my eyes and walked myself through the process.

Happy thoughts B, think happy thoughts. Favorite book. Favorite food. Favorite place. Miami. The beach. The sun. Relaxing in the sun on the beach in Miami. Relaxing in the sun on the beach in Miami with my favorite book eating my favorite food. God I love Miami. I can't wait to go back.

The more I lost myself in the thoughts of my favorite things, the calmer I became. My breathing returned to normal, and when I opened my eyes, the room was finally at a standstill. All of a sudden I was exhausted. My eyes were burning and my body felt insanely heavy. I took another deep breath, stood up and looked in the sink at that stupid stick. "I can't do this right now," I said out loud. "Fuck this shit. I'm going to bed."

I left the test in the sink, turned off the bathroom light and went to my bedroom. I crawled under my blankets.

Happy thoughts B. Relaxing in the sun on the beach in Miami with my favorite food.

. . .

I was rudely awakened by my bladder begging to be relieved and my Yorkie patting my arm. She was begging on behalf of her bladder.

I reached for my phone on the other side of the bed to check the time—10:37 A.M. I stumbled out of bed, into the bathroom and onto the toilet without turning on the light. When I was done peeing, I stayed on the toilet for an extra three minutes in my usual morning daze. My dog snapped me out of it when she came in barking.

"Alright man," I told her. "Jesus. I'm coming."

I stood up, switched on the light and turned to wash my hands and face, but stopped when I saw that fucking stick in the sink from the night before. I picked it up and looked at the two pink lines. "You again," I said throwing it into the garbage.

I washed up and brushed my teeth. I threw on a pair of sweats and took my dog outside to handle her business, and then came back in and called the doctor to schedule an appointment.

My mind was made up.

A week later, I walked into the waiting room and couldn't help but notice the ugly green and white walls. It wasn't a refreshing type of green. It was an ugly pasty green. It was gross, and I cringed as I sat and waited.

There were four other women there—one was with her boyfriend who was doing his best to try to console her as she cried, and the other three each had friends with them.

I was alone.

I had told my guy to wait in the car. I didn't feel there was any point in him being there. That place was uncomfortable enough as it was for me, and I would be even more uncomfortable with him present. As long as he was somewhere close-by, waiting, that was all that mattered to me. When the nurse came into the waiting area and called my name, I felt relieved that it was finally my turn, but I also felt fucked up about the fact that it was *my* turn. It was weird. I wanted to get it over with, but at the same time I felt guilty that I was in this situation to begin with. It was a fucking weird, icky and awkward combination of feelings.

I stood up and followed her down a long hallway covered with the same ugly green and into the other room.

Who the fuck would choose this color? For fuck sake!

We got into the room and the nurse handed me a hospital gown. In a very soft and comforting tone, she let me know that she was going to give me some privacy to change and that she would be back in a couple of minutes to bring me to the room where the procedure would take place.

I liked her. She had a soothing energy. "Will you be in the room with me for the procedure?" I asked. "I absolutely will. I'll be right beside you the entire time."

She left the room, and as I started to undress, I also started to cry. I didn't want a baby. I wasn't ready to be a mother, and this I knew. But even though I knew it and understood it, I still felt like shit. Being in this hospital, for this reason, made me feel like complete horse shit.

My phone vibrated in my back pocket. I pulled it out and read the text from my guy. "You okay?" I smiled through my tears at his sixth sense. "I'm okay," I texted back. "I'm going in right now. I'll message you when it's done."

He had been really supportive throughout this whole ordeal. We were on the same page and shared the same feelings. That helped a *whole* lot.

I finished undressing and had just put on the gown when the nurse came back for me. She took one look at me and knew that I had been crying. She took my hand and held it in hers. "Everything is going to be okay." she assured me sincerely. "The procedure is really quick and we put you to sleep. You won't feel or hear a thing. I promise."

I was glad she was my nurse. I was glad people like her, worked in places like this.

I nodded with understanding, and followed her once more to the next door over. In a gentle voice, she explained to me that I had to lay down, slide my bum to the end of the table (the same as if I were getting a checkup at the gyno) and that they were going to insert meds through my arm to put me to sleep. The doctor came in a second later, introduced himself, and also assured me that everything would be okay.

I nodded.

As I laid on the bed, waiting for the nurse to insert the needle into my arm, I felt my heart. And in my heart, I knew I was doing the right thing. In my heart, I knew I wasn't ready for the responsibilities of motherhood, and that was real. I wasn't prepared to gamble with the whole *"when the baby comes you'll know what to do"* thing—no fucking thanks.

Being a mother isn't a game. Being a mother is real life—a life I wasn't ready to live. Some people don't believe in abortions, and that's fine. When they become pregnant they can do whatever they want. I never thought of children as dolls. I know you can't give them back. It didn't matter how old I was—be it twenty-nine or thirty-five—if I wasn't ready, I wasn't ready, and that was that.

"I'm going to put the needle in your arm now," the nurse said. "Take a deep breath for me, it's going to pinch just a little." I inhaled deeply, felt a pinch, then exhaled. "Try your best to relax a bit. It won't be long before the medication sets in."

I looked over at the doctor as he prepared himself. I felt my nurse take my hand again and hold it in hers. I closed my eyes and I felt my body getting lighter. I went to a safe place, in my mind.

Happy thoughts B, happy thoughts—Favorite book. Favorite food. Favorite place to be. Miami. The beach. The sun. Relaxing in the sun on the beach in Miami.

Relaxing in the sun on the beach in Miami with my favorite book eating my favorite food. God I love Miami. I can't wait to go back...

"I think real peace comes from knowing in your heart that you've done what was best for you—not what your mom, your friends, or the outside world looking in thought was best—but what you thought was best, for you."

4

"Be honest," I said to him. "Would you take me back if I'd done even half of the things to you, that you've done to me?" Silently, he lowered his eyes to the ground. I shook my head. "Right. Didn't think so."

\#GetTheFuckOut

"Being good to him shouldn't hurt or drain you—if it does—there's something wrong. Maybe he's giving you bad in return for your good, or deep down, you know you're putting his wants above your own... and it's starting to catch up to your soul."

The sun beamed onto my face, waking me out of my sleep. I opened my eyes, squinted, and grabbed my phone from the night table to check the time—10:22am. I put the phone down and yawned. I had a million errands to run, plus I promised my mom a lunch date, so I needed to get my ass up and into the shower.

I'll just grab a coffee on the way I thought; as I calculated the time it would take me to get ready.

I was laying on my side when I felt his arm reach around me and his morning hard-on against my ass. "Good morning." He whispered into my ear. I rolled my eyes. *Gross.*

Everything about him had grossed me out for the past four months. He had become so unattractive to me that it had become a problem. It was a mixture of things that turned me off. He had been out of a job for nearly eight months, and I was holding down the house. I didn't mind picking him up while he was down *AT ALL*—that's what you do in a relationship. Duh! But there's a thin fucking line between tough times, and full out not doing anything to get *out* of those tough times.

Six months ago, he stopped looking for work all

together. Apparently, he officially decided to be a fulltime, stay-at-home, fucking loser... and I couldn't take it anymore. I worked two jobs, both were a forty-five minute drive from where we lived, two hours with traffic. I was paying two luxury car notes (his and mine) along with both insurances. I paid the rent, both of our phone bills, the cable, the light bill, the food, the EVERYTHING. I only had one day off a week and that day was reserved for running errands, grocery shopping and maybe a lunch with my mom and brothers. The other six days, I was out the door by noon and only walked back in at four in the fucking morning.

I was exhausted. Every part of my body hurt. I was working like crazy, but was *always* broke because every dime I made went to every bill we had. Then I'd come home at four in the morning and there he'd be, on the couch, with like eight of his friends in the house, playing fucking video games.

Might as well spit in my face.

I was fed up. And the fact that he wasn't making an effort to change the situation, was not only hurting my feelings, but turning me completely off towards him.

We argued about the same shit every three days. It

made no difference. Plus, it had been two months since I let his dick penetrate me—I didn't want it. I didn't even want to sleep in the same bed as him anymore, let alone fuck him. At this point, I didn't want him talking to me unless it was to say he found a *JOB*.

I didn't want to up and leave him because, well, you don't leave people when they're down and out. But at the same time, I felt like I was being used. I was being taken advantage of—and I was *fucking* tired.

I moved his arm away from me without being too rude and inched away from him. I didn't feel like starting the morning with an argument. My phone rang; it was my mom. I sat up and answered. "Hey mom, yes I'm up. I'm about to start getting ready right now." She laughed on the other end of the line. "Just checking babygirl. Call me when you're on your way. Love you." I smiled. "I love you back mom." I hung up and got out of the bed. "Where are you going?" He asked me.

"Lunch with my mom then errands," I replied dryly as put on my robe. "What kind of errands?"

Jesus fuck my life man would you just shut up?

That's what I wanted to say, but instead, I simply answered his question. "Dry cleaning, then I have to bring the car in for an oil change and have it checked at the same time. I keep hearing this weird knocking noise coming from the passenger side wheel. It's tripping me out. Then I gotta go to the bank. I'll come home, cook, and do the rest of the laundry after that."

I went to the dresser and grabbed my makeup bag. "Your attitude lately is disgusting," I heard him say from behind me. "You're miserable, you barely speak to me, I barely see you and I can't even get any pussy from my own damn woman."

...And just like that, the *no filter* switch went off in my brain. I put down the makeup bag, turned to face him, and yelled at the top of my lungs hurting my own ears.

"GET A FUCKING JOOOOOOOOOOB-AAAHH. What the fuck bro? You have SOME NERVE! I'm BUSTING my ass and I'M TIRED. YOU WATCH ME GO HARD EVERY SINGLE DAY FOR *US* while you sit around doing NOOOOTHING. I FUCKING HATE YOUR FACE LATELY okay? How about that? I fucking HATE your WHOLE face lately because you're not even bothering to TRY. I DON'T WANT TO BE WITH SOMEONE WHO IS COOL WITH WATCHING HIS WOMAN DO FUCKING EVERYTHING WHILE HE SITS WITH HIS FEET UP AND DOES FUCK ALL."

I clapped my hands in between words, "I. DON'T. WANT. TO. BE. WITH. A. MAN. LIKE. YOU."

It all happened so fast. There was no way I could have ever prepared for what came next.

He flew off of the bed, grabbed me by the neck with both of his hands and shoved me against the dresser. Instinctively, I put my own hands over his and tried to pry them off, but the more I tried, the harder he choked me.

"Who the fuck do you think you're talking to like that huh?!" was all he repeated with his face pressed against mine. I felt my throat closing up. All I could think was, *he's going to fucking kill me—right here, right now.*

He had never put his hands on me—no one had. I didn't know what to do, but I needed to do something quickly because it was very clear that in his fit of rage, he didn't give a fuck that I was about to lose consciousness. He squeezed my neck harder and harder every time he spoke; all of a sudden, he let go on his own. I fell to the floor, coughing, unable to process anything else. I just needed air.
He kneeled beside me and grabbed me in his arms, rocking me back and forth trying to sooth me.

"Oh my God! I'm so sorry B. I'm so sorry B. Oh my God, I swear I never meant to do that. I love you. I'm so sorry." I didn't give a fuck about what he was saying. I just needed to breathe.

I let him "comfort" me for a few minutes more until I felt I could stand again. I gave him a light push to signal that I needed space, and he moved away from me immediately, but held his hands out to help me as we stood up together. I was still wheezing a little. "I swear B, I fucking love you. I'm so sorry. You have to believe me." He said as he starting rubbing my back.

I faced him and looked into his eyes. There were tears in them, and they pleaded and begged for me to tell him it was okay, and that I forgave him.

Do you think I gave a flying fuck in hell about his tears or what his eyes were saying?

With all of my strength, I lifted my leg and kneed him as hard as I could right in his dick. He let out a groan of pain and hunched over as he cupped it. The second he was hunched over and vulnerable, I kneed him again—this time, clean in the mouth.

After that, I just fucking lost it.

I attacked him like a savage beast, kicking him anywhere I could. I didn't care, as long as my foot was making harmful contact with his body—that was all that mattered. He grabbed me to try to restrain me and yelled. "Stop it! Fucking stop!" But his efforts to restrain me only drove me more insane. He managed to get me in a position where my arms were locked by my side and he trapped me in something like a bear hug.

Do you think that stopped me? *Nope.*

The only weapons I had left were my teeth and the only part of his body I had access to was his face—so I bit it. I bit the side of his face as hard as I could and as he yelled out again in more pain, he had no choice but to let me go and back the entire fuck away from me. His face was bleeding and so was his mouth. He stood on one side of the room as I stood on the other, still trying to find more air. By then I was panting heavily, like a dog after a good run, and saliva leaked from the side of my mouth.

I wanted to speak. I wanted to tell him *"Don't you ever in your life think you can put your fucking hands on me and get away with that shit."* I wanted to tell him he was a little bitch for putting his hands on me. All because what? I HURT HIS FUCKING FEELINGS BY TELLING HIM THE TRUTH?!!!

But nothing came out of my mouth. I just stood there, panting, drooling, and staring straight at him.

I'm not sure what was on his mind.

The look on his face was mixed and it changed again and again. He looked upset because he was bleeding and physically hurt. Then he looked guilty as fuck. Then the look of guilt turned to extreme sadness. Suddenly, he looked freaked out, as if he didn't know what to say, or if he should speak at all, because he didn't know what else I was capable of.
And to be honest, in that moment, *I* didn't know what else I was capable of either. I wasn't scared of *him* at that point—I was scared of *me*.

Maybe the look on my face was "GET. THE. FUCK. OUT." because that's exactly what he did. I kept still, and followed him only with my eyes, as he grabbed the shirt he had worn the day before that laid on the pile of dirty laundry beside him, and put it on quickly. He kept on the sweatpants he had slept in, grabbed his car keys, and left without saying a word.

I on the other hand, was still frozen in place, even after he was gone, I couldn't move, or even cry.

I stood motionless, in complete shock.

I couldn't believe what just happened. I thought about the stories that I had heard, or seen on TV, or read in books about men hitting women, and all the times my girls and I sat around and said things like, "if that were me?! Shit, I would have..."

And now here I was, with my own fucking story.

A story I didn't want to have at all.

A story I didn't want to tell at fucking all.

You know we all say that, "If that were me, I would have..." shit. But the truth is, you have *no idea* how you're going to react or what you're *really* going to do, until you're actually face to face with some *bullshit*.

I heard my phone ringing.
I knew it was my mom, calling to ask where I was.
I closed my eyes and tried to drown out the sound.

I needed a moment to figure out what the fuck I was going to do from here.

"I wasn't always this way...
I used to be quite the pushover actually.
Super shy, extra quiet, afraid of speaking up
for myself, afraid of standing up for myself...
But life has groomed me into the woman I
am today—one who talks when she needs to,
and fights back when she has to."

x

5

"Maybe you're not the woman for him either though," she said. "And that doesn't take away from the woman you are. It doesn't make you inferior—it doesn't have to be a bad thing. It could simply mean that maybe you *are* too good for him, or that maybe, he's not ready for someone like you. Or maybe he wants someone who's less of a challenge—easier to manipulate and walk all over. Maybe he's got bad karma that's supposed to catch up to him, and the entire universe is working overtime to get you away from, and keep you out of that mess. It's not only them who aren't for us girl... sometimes, we ain't the ones for them either."

#ADiseaseCalledJealousy

"I don't even care about hurting a dude's ego anymore. If you ain't on my level, I'm gonna let you know that you ain't on my level—and if that shit hurts your little ego—use that hurt as fuel to step your fucking man game up."

It was around one in the morning when I pushed my key in the door.

I had been on the set of a photoshoot since four in the afternoon. My feet were killing me, fatigue burned my eyes, and I couldn't fucking wait to wash the seventy-three fucking pounds of makeup off of my face. I walked into our apartment, and all of the lights were on—such a fucking pet peeve.

Why does he need every single light in the house to be on? Why?

I set my bags on the floor and went to the living room to see if he had fallen asleep on the couch watching T.V. But he was still awake, sitting on the couch, laptop in hand surfing the Net.

"Hey babe," I said as I plopped down beside him and exhaled deeply. It felt good to finally be home after a long day. "Hey," he answered dryly without looking up at me.

Okaaay I thought to myself. *Rude much?*

"How was your day?" I asked.

"It was fine."

Again, he kept his eyes glued to the screen. His reply was just as dry as the first. I stretched my neck a bit so I could look at the screen to see what the fuck was so incredibly interesting that he couldn't take two fucking seconds to greet me properly.

He was on Facebook, scrolling through his newsfeed.

I spoke again—"Aren't you going to ask me how my day was?" He inhaled as if he was annoyed.

"How was your day B?"

Okay, I couldn't take it anymore.

"What's your problem?" I asked. He immediately shut the laptop and finally turned to face me. "Don't you think it's kind of late to be coming home from a photoshoot?"

Uuuuummm... was he serious right now? Like, was this a serious question he was asking me?

Last time I checked, I wasn't twelve years old and didn't have a fucking curfew. It's not like I was out running the streets—I was working for fuck's sake.

"I sent you a text at nine telling you the shoot was

going to run overtime. The makeup artist showed up an hour late, so by the time I got out of hair and makeup, the entire shoot was two hours behind schedule. I explained all of this to you already."

I was so confused.

He stared at me with a blank expression.

"What?!" I snapped.

"You're always working. If you don't have a shoot, you're at work pulling a twelve-hour shift. If you're not pulling a twelve-hour shift, you're in a meeting. If you're not in a meeting, you're locked in the bedroom writing. I feel like you're always working and I'm just here, waiting on you."

I immediately brought my palms to my head and started rubbing my temples.

This has to be a fucking joke right now.

There was no fucking way this man was actually sitting there, in my face, staring me dead in the eyes, complaining about me working yet again—impossible.

It was *impossible* to think that, instead of supporting my determination to make something of myself, he was shitting all over it for the millionth time.

I was exhausted. I didn't want to deal with him. If I opened my mouth to speak, the things that would've come out wouldn't have been very nice.

Let me just take my ass in the shower right now.

I left the couch without saying a word, and walked towards the bathroom.

"Oh, now you have nothing to say? Now who's the one with problem?"

His words hit my back. I stopped, turned to face him, and exploded. "You know what you are?" I asked with zero intent of letting him reply. "You're fucking ungrateful, and I'm going to tell you why." I took two steps closer to him. "I don't work mornings—you do—YET every fucking morning, do you not get your belly filled with a FULL course breakfast before you walk out that door? Who wakes up and cooks that for you? Oh, that would be me. Do you NOT come home EVERY night to a full course DINNER whether I'm here to eat it with you or not? Who spends the rest of the morning cooking that for you? Hmmm, oh yes! That would be ME again."

The more words I spat, the angrier I became, and the angrier I became, the louder I shouted.

"What is it with you?! It was all good when I was in the house most of the time though. Back when I wasn't going as hard as I am now, and only working a couple of days a week—that was okay. When you were going to work then kicking it with your boys until all hours of the night while I was home—*that* was okay though. A stay-at-home housewife with NO ring is cool with you. A woman who's out there hustling, trying to make something of herself and finally making some headway with it, isn't cool with you though. Right? I just don't get it. Maybe I would understand your argument if I was totally neglecting your needs, but I don't do that. I still cook, clean, spend my days off with you, ride your dick like a fucking pro every single morning or night, and you have the nerve to down talk me because I'm working? Talkin' about how you're just here, *waiting* for me?"

This is insane.

"What do you want me to do? Stop everything for you to be happy knowing I'm HOME? Are you mad because at this point I hustle HARDER than you? I don't get it. If that's the case, go get yourself a side hustle. Pick up a trade. Start a small business. Step UP to my level. I don't know about you, but I want way more out of life than what I have right now. I wanna build a life I can be proud of, and I'm sick and fucking tired of you forever making me feel like I'm wrong for that. Instead of always trying to pull me down to your miserable level, why don't you step yourself up to my *ambitious* level?"

I knew I had stepped all over his ego, but I didn't give a fuck. Enough was enough. Ever since I started taking my life and my goals seriously, he always had a fucking smart-ass almost jealous type of comment to make. I would get a call to do a photoshoot, and he would say, "Guess you're on your way to being a superstar huh?"—but with an attitude. I would get an article featured in a magazine, and he'd be like, "Guess everyone is gonna know your name now huh?"—with a fucking attitude. Man, why couldn't he be happy for me? Everything I had been working for was slowly starting to pay off, and he was always trying to make me feel bad about it.

"Get on your ambitious level?" he repeated.

He opened the laptop and resumed his previous activities as a way of dismissing the argument and me. He nodded his head, "Get on your ambitious level huh B?"

I didn't care. I was fucking over it.
I turned back around and made my way to the
bathroom. I turned on the water and peeled my clothes
off. Being drained and angry at the same time was a
horrible combination.
I got in the shower and the minute the hot water hit
my skin, I felt an overwhelming sadness inside me.

I was insecure about myself for so long—insecure and
afraid of so many things. I was afraid to chase my
dreams, afraid to take those first steps towards them,
afraid of the doors I'd have to knock down, afraid of
getting my writing out into the world, afraid of putting
myself out there—insecure and afraid.

I had to give myself so many fucking pep talks to get to
the place I was at, especially for the modeling shit,
because it wasn't what I loved. I didn't enjoy it much at
all because I hated cameras. But I had a pretty face and
my gigs were paid, and I figured that at the same time,
it would put me in front of people who were closer to
writing—and it did! I would get on set and get to
chitchatting with makeup artists and photographers
etc. They would ask me what else I did on the side, I'd
say writing, and they would often reply, "Oh I know
someone who works for ___ magazine, you should
send me your stuff. I know they're looking for a new
columnist."

And that's how I'd end up landing a lot of my writing gigs. I learned how to hustle efficiently; how to market myself efficiently. I learned how to speak up more and how to take initiative, and these things slowly built my confidence.

So there I was, finally confident and secure in my own skin. I liked myself. I loved myself. I was driven, hardworking, and had become the type to not let anything, or anyone, get in my way. Standing in the shower, I thought back to all the times he told me I was just 'too much,' or gave me attitude when I did something dope... and I started to understand what his problem was.

I was a constant reminder of everything he wasn't—and instead of being inspired to step himself up to my level—it was easier for him to try to break me back down to his. I was focused and fueled by my passions, and he hated it... and that shit hurt me.

How could I stay with someone like that?

I had always been warned about jealous friends wanting the life you live, but I had never been warned about jealous boyfriends wanting the life you live.

I guess this was my warning huh?

"It does fuck with you, because sometimes it's truly not your fault. You find yourself in almost the same situation, with a different guy, and it fucks with you. You could have sworn you did everything right this time. You looked for red flags and didn't find any. You took your time and let his actions speak louder than his words. You waited before you introduced him to your friends and family because you wanted to watch him first... you wanted to be sure, first. Then the moment you relaxed and felt like you covered all your bases—there he was with the switch up. There he was, bringing you back into the exact same shit you swore you'd never be in again... And that shit fucks with you. It really does."

✗

2

"Gawt damn B!" Erika said as she opened her front
door. "I'm only gonna say this cause I love you—but
you look like shit." I rolled my eyes and handed her my
ticket for the Drake concert we were all supposed to go
to that night. "Good to know that I look exactly how I
feel," I told her. She took the ticket, looked at it, and
looked back at me. "Girl, what is going on with you?
It's *gotta* be real if you're missing Drake. You love
Drake. Talk to me man." I shook my head. "I'm just
fucking tired yo. I need sleep, and like maybe four
boxes of Oreo cookies. I go to Drake's show every year,
missing one won't kill me." She raised her eyebrows.
"Alright, now I know you must be hella tired, cause the
B I know, doesn't say things like 'missing Drake's show
won't kill me.' She laughed, and made me crack a small
smile. "I'll be alright. Y'all go and have a good time."
"You sure you don't want my sister to pay you for this
ticket?" she asked. "I mean, at least it won't be a total
waste." — "Nah, it's all good. I'm happy to gift it to
her." Erika put her arms out and gave me a hug. "Get
that rest. We'll call you in the morning boo."

#TimeOut

"Yes, I know that I'll be fine and eventually things will work themselves out. I know what is meant for me will always be for me—I know. But sometimes I need a minute or two to pull myself together, because sometimes, the shit life throws at me gets a little hectic... that's all."

"You have four new messages, and two saved messages. To listen to your new messages, press one now."

I obeyed the lady on my voicemail, and pressed one.

"First new message"

"Hey girl, where you at, where you aaaaat? Call me."

"Next new message"

"Yo yo yo. Is your phone broken or something? It's not like you to not be answering your phone or texts. Hit me back or I'm calling Mom."

"Next new message"

"Baby girl, it's mommy. I'm starting to get worried now. A couple of the girls called here saying that you've been unreachable and I know you like to go M.I.A sometimes when you're not feeling well. So if that's what this is, then just at least send me a text to say that you're alive and I'll pass the message along. I love you babygirl."

"Next new message"

"Good afternoon, this message is for Miss Cici. B from Bell Canada in regards to your late paym..."

"Message deleted. End of new messages."

I laid in my bed and stared at the ceiling—something I had been doing for the last three days.

I knew I had to at least call my mom. I could understand the real worry that was probably starting to spread through her and my friends, and I didn't want anyone to think I was dead... even though that's exactly how I felt.

I groaned as I sat up and dialed her number. She answered on the first ring. "Babygirl." She said relieved. "Everything okay?" I was blessed with a mother I could literally tell anything to, but I didn't feel like explaining my emotions, at all.

"Hi mom. Yes, I'm alive. I'm just not feeling well. I broke the screen on my phone a couple days back, so I can't see any text messages and I don't feel like talking to anyone on the phone—that's all."
There was a short pause. I knew she was thinking of the right thing to say.

"Well," she finally started, "I figured you were going

through your own thing. I know how you get. I'll call the girls and let them know you're fine before they start ringing your doorbell. I won't keep you on the phone, but you know I'm here if you need me, and so is everyone else who loves you very much. Whatever you're going through, you'll get through it. You always do babygirl."

I smiled a little.

"Thanks mom. I love you. I'll talk to you soon."

We hung up and I laid right back down. My room was dark even though the clock on my nightstand read 2:17pm. I hadn't bothered to open the curtains.
I didn't feel like seeing the sun, and I didn't want the windows open to let in the sounds of summer either.
I didn't fucking feel like moving at all. I had spent the last three days in my dark room, watching movies.

I needed to be completely alone.

I wasn't well, mentally, emotionally, and spiritually. I felt drained in all areas. Why? Because I was overworked, struggling and stressed.

I had like 46382847 immediate bills to pay, was trying to fund my business projects at the same time, all while trying to *live* a little at the same time—which was almost impossible—because I was working non-fucking-stop. The crazy part was, with all of my soul, I knew everything I was doing, and everything I was working for, was eventually all going to pay off one day. It wasn't faith I lacked. It was the "eventually" part that was fucking killing me. I would get home late at night after work, and sometimes look up at the sky and whisper—"Hello? Do you see me down here? Is it eventually yet, or no?"

I had always been someone who stayed away from others when I wasn't feeling well. When I wasn't feeling well, I couldn't talk or think about anything else.

The shit consumed me.

I'm an extremist. If I'm happy, I'm all the way consumed with happiness. If I'm sad, I'm all the way consumed by my sadness—no middle ground.

Shutting all the way down and crawling into my own little hole, and staying there until I was ready to come out, was just who I was. I always felt like I didn't want to burden my friends and family with my shit, so I just kept to myself.

So there I was, alone in my little hole, declaring a time-out. No phone, no people, no outside world, no work, nothing at all—just me in bed, recharging all of my batteries.

Everyone has their own way of dealing with things. That just happened to be mine. I think sometimes the hardest thing about life is trying to keep your head on your shoulders while you're going through it. I do my best, I swear to God I do, but every now and then, man—I just need a break.

You know?

I just needed a fucking break.

"I've learned not to ask for permission to take time for myself. This is my body, my soul, my heart, and my mind—and though my track record has proven that, I am indeed strong and can handle a lot—I am not fucking superwoman.
I need my rest when I need my rest."

✗

Own Your Truths x *Set Yourself Free*

By now it's no secret, I am extremely vulnerable, raw, and brutally honest when it comes to my writing. And I know with that comes a huge window of opportunity for others to judge the entire shit out of me—but I'm cool with it.

I know who am.

I know why I've made the choices I've made in my life.

And I know where those very choices, good and bad, have lead me...

Right here.

All of the shit I've been through, and sometimes willingly put myself through, helped me to find my courage, my strength, and my voice. But I'm not a life coach, advisor, therapist, or a relationship guru, nor do I ever want to be.

I write stories about what I've done, haven't done, should have done, and learned—and if reading my shit can help women get through their own shit, or inspire them to never want to be in the shit I've been in, then hey, I guess I'm doing exactly what I'm supposed to be doing. I guess in retrospect, all of the negative parts of my life were simply setting me up for a mass positive.

Every woman has her story. I just happen to be okay
with sharing so many of mine.
I've lost and found myself a million times, only to lose
and find myself all over again.

This is life, and it is what it is. Shit is gonna happen.
It's gonna get complicated. We're gonna relapse.
We're gonna need time-outs. We're gonna be weak.
We're gonna be strong. We're gonna lose our shit and
yell for people to get the fuck out of our lives. We're
gonna break down and beg some people to stay in our
lives. Some days we're gonna feel everything all at once.
Other days, we're gonna feel nothing at all. We're
gonna be in some bad spaces, we're gonna be in some
amazing ones. We're gonna get on our knees crying and
hurting and praying for help. We're gonna get on our
knees and pray just to say thank you. We're gonna have
moments when we know exactly what we want, and
we're sure. We're gonna have moments when we legit
have no fucking clue what we want, and we're
confused.

This life shit isn't a movie, and I think sometimes, we
forget that. Sure we can ride off into the sunset one
night with our hair blowing perfectly in the wind, with
the love of our lives by our sides, and we can have the
best friends in the world. But the next morning, or the
morning after that, we can just as easily wake up to

pouring rain, no umbrella, some fucked up hair, friends who betrayed us out of nowhere, and the love of our lives fucking gone. Unlike the end of the movie, real life keeps going, so we have to keep going too.

I remember at one point in my life, I was constantly searching for the easy way out of shit. I ran from my problems, swept them under the rug, pretended I was okay ALL the time, and acted like things didn't really get to me. But there came a point when I had to fucking stop. I had to stop searching for an easy way out, and realize that whatever was thrown my way, was meant for me—no matter what it was, how hard it was, or how much I didn't like it. I had to get a grip of myself, be as brave as I could be, and deal with it the best way I knew how.

I've made some really smart moves throughout my life, and I've also made some really fucking dumb ones. I've repeated some of the same mistakes a good twenty miserable times before I finally learned my fucking lesson—and so what? Does that make me a bad person? Does it make me any less deserving of healthy love, good things, and good people around me? Fucking no. What it makes me, is a gawt damn woman on her own journey towards *her* purpose in this world.

Owning all of my truths has set me free from a lot of

things. If anything, I hope I've inspired you to own yours too.

Much love,

B

Lost And Found

The Book Of Short Stories

Cici. B

Twitter-Facebook-Instagram @TheCrimsonKiss